www.readtosucceed.org
615-738-7323

STOP! LOOK! LISTEN!

How Do Elephants Stay Safe at School?

For all of the students at Brown's Chapel Elementary...

Top Row (L to R): Mrs. Amanda Henry, Jessica DeLambert, Gabriella Derchy, Tyler Knox, Gabriella Phillips, Destinee Miller, S.R.O. Bill West, Mrs. Kimberly Barlow

Middle Row: Albert Kupchik, Chloe Laird, Zachary Joyce, Ezekiel Hicks, Sierra Brauchi, Sera Brauchi, Rylee Jackson, Mrs. Jenna Rose

Front Row: Chloe Chauffe, Micah Buckley, Jack Cashion, Ellie Burton, Ian Qualls, Jayden Allen

Not Pictured: Karson Bostian, Sadie Burton

How do elephants stay safe in a fire?

Does an elephant run around in shock?
Does he stay in and play with the clock?

Does an elephant cover up the alarm?
Does she play with the toy farm?

Does an elephant stay and read some books?
Does he party with the cafeteria cooks?

How do elephants stay safe in bad weather?

Does an elephant freak out and go outside?
Does she run around and hide?

Does an elephant stand on the windowsill?
Does he jump up and down and squeal?

Does an elephant do the jungle stomp?
Does she do the rain forest romp?

No! An elephant will **STOP** and **LOOK** at his teacher.
He will **LISTEN** like a respectful creature.

How do elephants stay safe during a lock down?

Does an elephant paint the bad guy?
Does he offer him some homemade strawberry pie?

Does an elephant greet the stranger, "Hello"?
Does he go and eat a big white marshmallow?

School Safety Rules and Tips

As long as you follow these three simple rules, you will be able to handle any emergency that comes your way.

1. STOP - Stop what you are doing when you hear an alarm.

2. LOOK - Look at your teacher or other adult who is in charge of you.

3. LISTEN - Listen for instructions and remain calm.

In order to do this well we must
PRACTICE, PRACTICE, PRACTICE!

For Fire, Weather, or Lockdown Emergencies, just
STOP, LOOK, LISTEN!

STOP, LOOK, LISTEN!

(To the tune of "Jingle Bells")

Verse 1:
Sitting in math class
I guess I fell asleep
They just called a drill
No more counting sheep
Bad weather on the way
Our teacher leads us out
Crouch down by the wall
And please don't scream and shout.

Chorus:
Stop and look, stop and look,
Listen the whole time.
Your teacher wants to keep you safe,
So open up your eyes!
Stop and look, stop and look,
Listen the whole time.
Your teacher wants to keep you safe,
So open up your eyes!

Verse 2:
We're playing basketball
In the big old stinky gym
I hear the fire drill
And follow our coach, Tim
We walk in a straight line
He takes us all outside
No talking is allowed
'Cause there is such a big crowd

(Sing Chorus)

Verse 3:
Walking with my class
I hear the lockdown bell
All the students pass
To the nearest room
I'm a little scared
But I know just what to do
I find a hiding spot
And I hope that you do too!

(Sing Chorus)

CPSIA information can be obtained at www.ICGtesting.com
Printed in the USA
LVIW01n1423260815
451620LV00022B/224